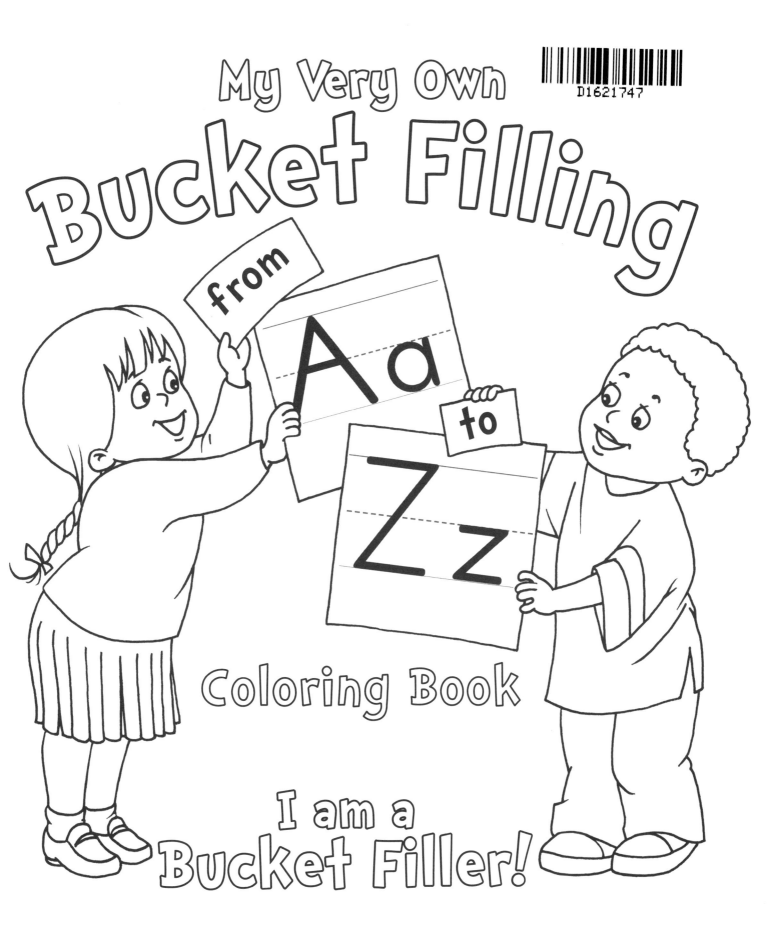

My Very Own Bucket Filling

from

Aa

to

Zz

Coloring Book

I am a Bucket Filler!

D1621747

My name is: _____

Be kind and be a bucket filler

Don't be mean and dip

You can fill buckets from A to Z

A a

Ask if you can help

Be a bucket filler

Cc

Cheer up a friend

Dd Donate to a special group

E e

Excited to fill buckets

Friends have fun or hang out

Gg Give a little of your time

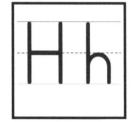

Heroes look out for others

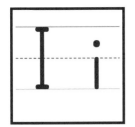 **Invite someone to join the fun**

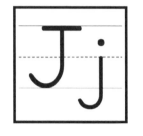

Joyful when you give a hug

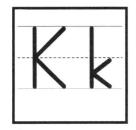

kindness brightens your day

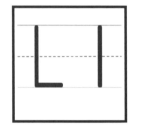

Listen when people talk

 Make a bucketfilling card

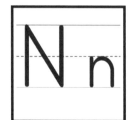

Notice helpful things

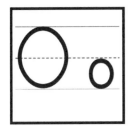

Offer to help

Pp

Practice daily bucket filling

Quit any bucket dipping

R r

Respect everyone

S s Smile and see what happens

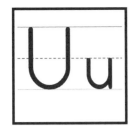

Use kind words

V v Volunteer to do some work

Ww

Watch out for bucket dipping

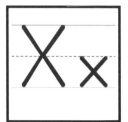

EXtra-special is a friend

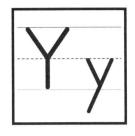

You do your best

Zz Zero you can't work out

Share these bucketfilling tips

How many ways can you fill buckets?

Use this checklist to keep track of all the ways
you can fill buckets from **A** to **Z**!

- [ ] Ask if you can help
- [ ] Be a bucket filler
- [ ] Cheer up a friend
- [ ] Donate to a special group
- [ ] Excited to fill buckets
- [ ] Friends have fun or hang out
- [ ] Give a little of your time
- [ ] Heroes look out for others
- [ ] Invite someone to join the fun
- [ ] Joyful when you give a hug
- [ ] Kindness brightens your day
- [ ] Listen when people talk
- [ ] Make a bucketfilling card
- [ ] Notice helpful things
- [ ] Offer to help
- [ ] Practice daily bucket filling
- [ ] Quit any bucket dipping
- [ ] Respect everyone
- [ ] Smile and see what happens
- [ ] Tell your family you love them
- [ ] Use kind words
- [ ] Volunteer to do some work
- [ ] Watch out for bucket dipping
- [ ] EXtra-special is a friend
- [ ] You do your best
- [ ] Zero you can't work out